What others are saying about the
REAL Phonics Reading Program

"This series provides parents with a high-quality reading curriculum consistent with the recommendations of the National Reading Panel. So many children fail to learn to read well. Following the program outlined in this series will help parents and teachers succeed in their efforts to teach young children to read. Well written and a must-have resource for parents and teachers alike."

— Gwenette R. Ferguson, Member U.S. National Reading Panel (NRP); Past Principal B. C. Elmore Middle School, Houston; Reading Teacher.

"If I had a child this age, I would use this book. I realize not everyone is as concrete and sequential as I am, but I recommend you just take this, and go all the way through it, and you will be amazed."

— Nancy Janney, Iowa Homeschool Supervisor; Teacher.

"I didn't want Emma getting bored in her second year of preschool, so I thought it would be great to start learning some kindergarten concepts before she actually started school. I was pretty shocked that she was reading a few pages into Book 1. I was really surprised with how quickly she caught on and would say it was a very good head start for kindergarten. Now she brings home a book a day from her kindergarten class and a book a week from the library."

— Jennifer Weestrand, Mother of three, Lakeville, Mn.

"Getting a head start on literacy is always a good idea... [REAL Phonics] is a fine pick for any educator or parent of a young child looking for resources to help teach kids how to read.

— Children's Bookwatch

How to Teach Your Child to Read With *REAL Phonics*™

If Possible, Start With Book 1

The Book 1 reading lesson plans are designed to teach your child important reading strategies that cannot be learned by reading trade books alone. Your child will learn to automatically identify vowels within words and sound out words with short vowel sounds. The short vowels require more practice than long vowels, and beginning phonics blending is much easier when the long vowels are saved for later. Book 1 will guide you and your child through 97 stories with all short vowel sounds.

> Short Vowels: tap, ten, rid, not, cub
> Long Vowels: tape, teen, ride, note, cube

Your young reader will also begin to discern root words from suffixes. Familiarity with root words and suffixes will enhance his or her ability to see patterns within words, as in bat, bats and batting.

If you have a struggling reader who is not making adequate progress in school, Book 1 will provide short vowel and phonics blending practice far beyond what he or she has encountered in regular reading classes. This is your chance to back up and get a fresh start. Most reading intervention programs focus on phonics because it works.

Real Phonics is perfect for gifted eduction. Gifted children love the stories, characters, color, logical progression and quick pace.

Using Book 2

The writing worksheets will help your child learn to read by incorporating the sense of touch into the lessons. If you skip over the handwriting worksheets during your one-on-one tutoring sessions, your child should return to them later and complete the writing practice. All of the worksheets in this book are available for free download at BrodenBooks.com.

Long vowels are introduced sequentially. Save the long vowel flash cards until they are called for.

Do all the drills. The question and answer drills are your opportunity to assess your child's progress. The drills are designed to reinforce all concepts to the point of automaticity. Children like repetition and you will appreciate the rapid learning that takes place with this method. The sequential advancement of the drills and stories set *REAL Phonics* apart from other phonics curricula.

The basic phonics rules taught in this program are foundational for homeschooling families, and a valuable addition to classroom reading instruction, summer reading programs, reading interventions and remedial reading programs.

Learn to Read
with
REAL Phonics

Homeschool Version, Book 2
For Beginning Readers

Written by Kallie Woods
Sketches by Courtney Huddleston
Ink & Color by Luisiana Araujo

Broden Books
Minneapolis, Minnesota

LEARN TO READ with REAL PHONICS
HOMESCHOOL VERSION, BOOK 2
FOR BEGINNING READERS
First Edition

Copyright © 2012 by Broden Books, Minneapolis, Minnesota

REAL Phonics is a trademark of Broden Books, LLC., Minneapolis, Mn.

Stock Art from Fotolia.com

Publisher's Cataloging-in-Publication Data
Woods, Kallie.
    Learn to read with real phonics : homeschool version.
    Book 2 / written by Kallie Woods; sketches by Courtney
    Huddleston; inks and color by Luisiana Araujo.
    --1st ed.
      p. cm.
    SUMMARY: Beginning phonics reading lessons teach
    children to sound out words containing long and short
    vowel sounds, by means of ninety-three illustrated short
    stories with on-page instructions for teachers.
      Audience: Ages 5-7.
      LCCN 2011943901
      ISBN 978-0-9832023-2-5

    1. Readers (Primary). 2. Reading--Phonetic method.
    3. Animals--Juvenile fiction. 4. Animals--Fiction.
    I. Title.

    PE1119.W66 2012   428.6

Published by Broden Books, LLC.
Minneapolis, Minnesota
www.BrodenBooks.com

Printed in the United States of America

Table of Contents

Underlying Principles of the REAL Phonics Reading Program

Beginning Reading Books for Homeschooling

REAL Phonics™ is a method of teaching children to read by sounding out words in controlled vocabulary stories, using basic phonics rules.

1) **Stories** are fun and motivational for beginning readers, but trade books do not provide the structure, repetition and incremental advancement needed for teaching children to read well. The *REAL Phonics* kindergarten reading curriculum provides all the fun of trade books, but in an organized format with each new concept in the proper sequence with the right amount of repetition.

2) **Repetition** may be boring for some adults, but young children love it and learn by it. The *REAL Phonics* reading program calls for teaching reading through constant repetition and over-learning of the phonics lessons and related concepts, such as punctuation, suffixes and syllables.

3) **Phonemic Awareness**, according to the report of the National Reading Panel, leads to improved reading comprehension, reading and spelling. This series places great emphasis on phonemic awareness. Any child who can sound out the word "cat" is aware of the three phonemes involved. Children who learn to sight read are far less aware of phonemes. The *REAL Phonics* method keeps sight words to a bare minimum at the outset, as they can be much more easily acquired after the child has learned to sound out words phonetically.

4) **Dolch word lists** and other lists of sight words aim to foster automatic recognition of words without sounding them out. *Real Phonics,* on the other hand, teaches decoding and phonics blending skills that can be used whenever a new word is encountered. Automaticity will develop naturally with repetition and experience.

5) **Short vowels** are much more difficult to learn than long vowels. Beginning readers should be allowed the luxury of reading many easy stories containing only short vowels. Long vowel words should be introduced only after the short vowels have been mastered.

6) **Simple spelling exercises** help develop the ability to visualize words.

7) **Technical terms,** like apostrophe, syllable, root word, suffix and exclamation point, need not be memorized by young readers, but children should be able to identify and interpret these elements when they see them in print. We ask, "How many syllables does 'roses' have?" so that the student will learn to see and hear the separate syllables, not so she will learn the technical term.

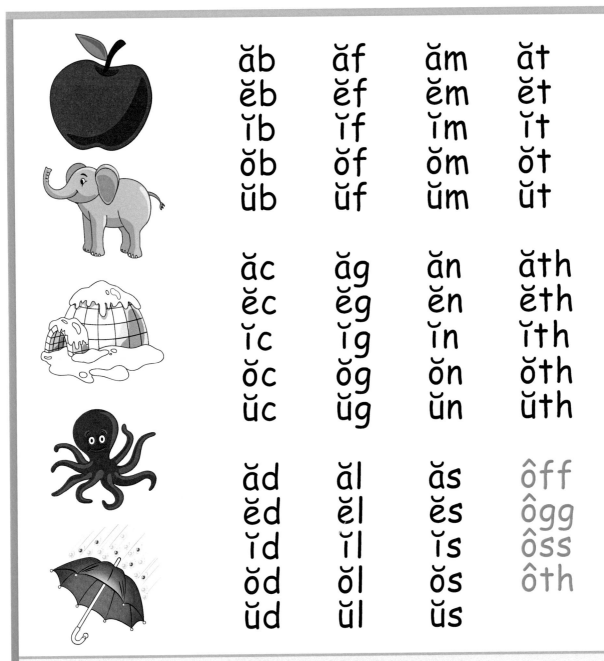

ăb	ăf	ăm	ăt
ĕb	ĕf	ĕm	ĕt
ĭb	ĭf	ĭm	ĭt
ŏb	ŏf	ŏm	ŏt
ŭb	ŭf	ŭm	ŭt
ăc	ăg	ăn	ăth
ĕc	ĕg	ĕn	ĕth
ĭc	ĭg	ĭn	ĭth
ŏc	ŏg	ŏn	ŏth
ŭc	ŭg	ŭn	ŭth
ăd	ăl	ăs	ôff
ĕd	ĕl	ĕs	ôgg
ĭd	ĭl	ĭs	ôss
ŏd	ŏl	ŏs	ôth
ŭd	ŭl	ŭs	

Reviewing the Short Vowels

1. **Review** these Book 1 flash cards: Ă, Ĕ, Ĭ, Ŏ, Ŭ, Ô. It is very important to thoroughly learn the short vowel sounds before beginning the long vowels.

2. *__Point__* to "ab, eb, ib, ob, ub" and read them to your student, rhyming with "dab, web, rib, rob, rub."

3. Continue reading and pointing rather rapidly. Make sure you rhyme "off, ogg, oss, oth" with "off,

hog, toss, cloth."

4. Now have your student read the syllables. Make sure "as, es, is" rhymes with "lass, less, miss."

5. Return to this page as needed to reinforce the short vowel sounds.

Ā, ā	tăp, tāpe măt, māte hăt, hāte răt, rāte	măn, māne căn, cāne făd, fāde păn, pāne	
Ē, ē	tĕn, tēen rĕd, rēed bĕt, bēet fĕd, fēed	wĕd, wēed mĕt, mēet pĕp, pēep stĕp, stēep	bē hē mē wē
Ī, ī	rĭd, rīde hĭd, hīde rĭp, rīpe wĭn, wīne	dĭm, dīme pĭn, pīne bĭt, bīte fĭn, fīne	hī
Ō, ō	nŏt, nōte rŏd, rōde rŏb, rōbe rŏt, rōte	cŏd, cōde dŏt, dōte tŏt, tōte	gō nō sō
Ū, ū	cŭb, cūbe mŭtt, mūte cŭt, cūte fŭss, fūse	tŭb, tūbe dŭd, dūde	

Phonics Sound Chart for Long and Short Vowels

1. Explain that a straight line over a vowel means it has the long sound. Long vowels sound just like the letter names.

2. **Long O**: Point at Long O and say: "Long O sounds like 'oh' as in 'ok.'" Point to the E's on the ends of the words and say, "This is Silent E. It's crossed out because it has no sound. Silent E makes the other vowel have the long sound. Sound out "not" then "note," "rod" then "rode," etc. Point at the words "go," "no," and "so," and explain that a vowel on the end of a word is long.

3. **Proceed to page nine.** Do not teach the rest of the long vowels until they appear in the stories. It is easier to learn the long vowels one at a time.

Long A: Point at Long A and say: "Long A sounds like 'ay' as in 'angel.' Point at "tape" and ask, "What does Silent E do to the A?" (It makes it long). Sound out the long and short A words, defining each word as you go.

Long E: Point at Long E and say: "Long E sounds like 'ee' as in 'eagle.'" Point at "teen" and say, "When two vowels are together, the first one is usually long and the second one is silent." Remind your student that a vowel on the end of a word is usually long. Sound out the long and short E words, defining each word as you go.

Long I: Point at Long I and say: "Long I sounds like 'eye' as in 'ice cream.'" Sound out the I words.

Long U: Point at Long U and say: "Long U sounds like 'you' as in 'unicorn.'" Don't make an issue out of the fact that "cube" and "mute" are phonetically "kyoob" and "myoot," while "dude" and "tube" sound like "dood" and "toob." Sound out the U words.

Go Dog!

Dan hits a ball.

The ball goes in the mud!

That dog goes in the mud and gets the ball.

Go dog! Go!

Long O Sound & Rule for Two Vowels Together

1. *If you skipped Book 1 ask:* "What are the five vowels?"

   (A, E, I, O, U)

2. Find all the vowels in the 3rd panel.

3. Sound out the first new word.

4. *Point* at the second new word and say: "The rule for two vowels together is: the 'first one is long and the second one is silent.'"

5. Sound out the second new word and read the story.

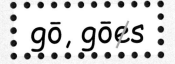

gō, gōes

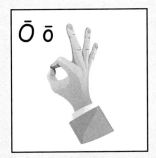

Ō ō

The Dog

Is that Bella?

The dog goes to Bella.

Is that Matt?

The dog goes to Matt.

Review

1. Practice with your flash cards for long O and the letters and sight words that were learned in Book 1:

Ă, Ĕ, Ĭ, Ŏ, Ŭ, Ô, Ō, to, of, the
N, T, S, D, H, C, R, M, TH, F, B, L, G

2. DO NOT practice with the flash cards for any long vowels other than Ō at this time. A common mistake is to introduce the long vowels too quickly, causing the beginning reader to confuse the long and short vowel sounds.

3. Read the story.

4. Proceed to page 11. Read the page aloud together, then let your student trace the gray letters in a top-down direction. The writing practice is part of the reading lesson and should not be skipped. Download extra copies of page 11 and all of the writing practice pages at BrodenBooks.com.

Writing Practice

go ~~go   go~~

goes ~~goes   goes~~

The dog goes to Bella.

~~The dog goes to Bella.~~

The dog goes to Matt.

~~The dog goes to Matt.~~

Is that Bella?

~~Is that Bella?~~

Is that Matt?

~~Is that Matt?~~

Learn to Read with REAL Phonics, Book 2
By Kallie Woods
© 2012 Broden Books, LLC., Minneapolis, Mn. USA

The Dog Goes Fast

Ann's dog ran fast.

The dog ran past Ann.

Can Ann go fast?

Ann can not get the dog.

Learning to Read - The "ST" Sound

1. ***If you skipped Book 1 ask:*** "What are the 5 vowels?"

   (A, E, I, O, U)

2. ***If you skipped Book 1 ask:*** "What is a consonant?"

   (Any letter that is not a vowel)

3. ***Ask:*** "Are S and T consonants?"

(Yes!)

4. ***Point*** at the star and explain that the consonants S and T together have the "sst" sound as in "star."

5. Sound out the new words, find the ST's in the story, then read the story.

St, st

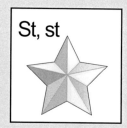

fắst, pắst

Ann Gets the Dog

The dog ran to Bella.

The dog goes past Bella.

The dog ran past Dan.

Ann got the dog.

Review

1. Practice with your flash cards:

   to, of, the

2. *Ask:* "How do you spell 'to?'"

   (T-O)

3. Find the word "to" in the story.

4. *If you skipped Book 1 ask:* "What are the five vowels?"

   (A, E, I, O, U)

5. *Ask:* "What letter has to be in every word?" (A vowel)

6. *Ask:* "What is a consonant?"

(Any letter that's not a vowel)

7. *Point* at the word "goes" in the 2nd panel and ask: "What is the rule for two vowels together?"

   (The first one is usually long, the second one is silent)

8. Read the story.

The Ball Goes Fast

This big rat has a bat.

That cat has a ball.

The big rat hits the ball to the cat.

The ball goes past the cat!

Review

1. ***If you skipped Book 1 ask:*** "What does an exclamation point mean?"

    (Surprise or excitement)

2. Find the exclamation point in the story.

3. ***Point*** at the word "goes" in the fourth panel and ask: "What is the rule for two vowels together?"

    (The first one is usually long, the second one is silent)

4. Read the story together with the proper inflection for the exclamation point.

5. ***If you skipped Book 1 ask:*** "What are the five vowels?"

    (A, E, I, O, U)

"What is a consonant?"

    (Any letter that is not a vowel)

"What letter has to be in every word?"

    (A vowel)

A Mad Cat

Can the cat run to the ball?

The cat runs fast.

The cat has the ball.

The ball falls! The cat is mad.

Suffixes and Root Words

1. **_Point_** at the new words and ask, "What vowel is in the new words?" (Short U)

2. Sound out the new words.

3. **_If you skipped Book 1:_** Point at "runs" and explain that the S on the end of "runs" is a suffix. A suffix goes on the end of a word. We call the original word the "root word" and we call the ending the "suffix."

4. Find the question mark and the exclamation point in the story.

5. Read the story.

Note: Identifying the root word helps your student see patterns in words.

rŭn
rŭns

Will the Ant Go In?

This ant goes in the hill.

Lots of ants will go in the hill.

That ant has a hat on.

Will that ant go in the hill?

Learning to Read - The Letter W

1. ***Point*** at the new letter and say, "This is W and it has the 'wuh' sound as in 'watermelon.'"

2. Say the "wuh" sound together.

3. ***Ask:*** "What vowel is in the new word?" (Short I)

4. ***Ask:*** "What does short I sound like?"

(Like 'ĭh' as in 'igloo')

5. Sound out the new word and read the story.

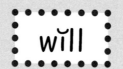

wĭll

W, w

The Hat on the Hill

The ant goes in the hill.

The ant goes in and the hat falls off.

His hat will not go in the hill.

The hat falls off of the hill.

Easy Spelling Words

1. Practice with your flash cards for the following letters. Show the letter side first, and ask for the letter sound. Don't show the picture side unless your student needs a hint.

    Ă, Ĕ, Ĭ, Ŏ, Ŭ, Ô, Ō, N, T, S, D, H, C, R
    M, TH, F, B, L, G, ST, W, to, of, the

2. *Ask:* "How do you spell 'to?'" (T-O)

3. *Ask:* "How do you spell 'of?'" (O-F)

4. *Ask:* "How do you spell 'the?'" (T-H-E)

5. *Point* at "goes" in the first panel and ask: "What is the rule for two vowels together?" (The first one is usually long, the second one is silent)

6. Read the story.

Note: Simple spelling exercises help develop your student's ability to visualize words.

Up the Hill

Bella has a bat.

Dan has a ball.

Bella hits the ball up.

The ball goes up on the hill.

Learning to Read - The Letter P

1. **_Point_** at the pirate and explain that P has the "pp" sound, as in pirate. Say the "pp" sound together.

2. Sound out the new word and read the story.

3. Proceed to the next page and read the word list together, then allow your student to trace the gray words with a pencil.

ŭp

P, p

Writing Practice

fast   fast   fast

past   past   past

run   run   run

runs   runs   runs

will   will   will

hill   hill   hill

up   up   up

Dan runs.   Dan runs.

The ant goes in the hill.

The ant goes in the hill.

Learn to Read with REAL Phonics, Book 2
By Kallie Woods
© 2012 Broden Books, LLC., Minneapolis, Mn. USA

A Small Ant

This is a small ant.

This small ant has a small ball.

That is a big ant.

That big ant has a big ball.

Learning to Read - The SM Sound

1. **_Point_** at the smiley face and explain that the consonants S and M together have the "sm" sound, as in "smile."

2. Say the "sm" sound together.

3. **_Point_** at the new word and explain that the A has the "aw" sound, as in "awning."

4. Sound out the new word and read the story.

Ô small

Sm, sm

20

The Balls Go Up

This small ant bats the small ball.

The small ball goes up.

The big ant bats the big ball.

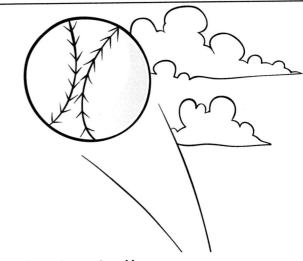

The big ball goes up.

Alphabet Flash Card Review

1. Practice with your flash cards for the following letters. Show the letter side first, and ask for the letter sound. Do not show the picture side unless your student needs a hint.

Ă, Ĕ, Ĭ, Ŏ, Ŭ, Ô, Ō
ST, W, P, SM, the, to, of

2. *Ask:* "How do you spell 'to?'" (T-O)

3. *Ask:* "How do you spell 'of?'" (O-F)

4. *Ask:* "How do you spell 'the?'" (T-H-E)

5. *Point* at "goes" in the second panel and ask: "What is the rule for two vowels together?"

(The first one is usually long, the second one is silent)

6. Read the story.

A Can of Bones

Ann has a big can.

The can has lots of bones in it.

All the bones fall.

A hill of bones.

Long O, Silent E

1. Review the O section on page 8.

2. **_Point_** at the first new word and ask: "What does the straight line mean over the O?"

   (It means the O is long)

3. **_Ask:_** "Why is the E crossed out?" (Because it's silent)

4. **_Ask:_** "What does Silent E do to the other vowel?"

   (It makes it long)

5. Sound out the new words together and read the story.

6. **_Point_** at "bones" and ask:

"What is the suffix?" (s)

"What is the root word?" (bone)

bōne
bōnes

The Dog Runs Home

Can the dog get a bone?

Ann hands the dog a bone.

The dog bit on the bone.

The dog goes home.

New Word

1. **_Point_** at the word 'goes' in the fourth panel and ask: "What is the rule for two vowels together?"

   (The first one is usually long, and the second one is silent)

2. **_Point_** at the new word "home" and ask, "What are the vowels in this new word?"

   (Long O, Silent E)

3. **_Ask:_** "Why is the E silent?"

   (Because it's on the end of the word)

4. **_Ask:_** "Why is the O long?"

   (Because of the silent E)

5. Sound out the new word.

6. Find the question mark and read the story.

Dan's Fire

Dan has a fire.

He sits on a log.

Ann and Bella sit on the log.

Bella hands Ann a hotdog.

Long I - Our First Compound Word

1. **_Point_** at the ice cream and say, "This is long I. It sounds like 'eye' as in 'ice cream.'" Then teach the I section on page 8.

2. **_Point_** at the first new word and ask: "What does the straight line mean over the I?" (The I is long)

3. **_Ask:_** "Which letter in this word is silent?" (E)

4. **_Ask:_** "What does Silent E do to the I?" (It makes it long)

5. Sound out the first two words.

6. **_Point_** at "hotdog" and explain that a compound word is made of two smaller words.

7. Sound out "hotdog" and read the story.

fīrę, lŏg, hŏt|dŏg

Ann Tosses the Hotdog

Ann has hotdogs.

The fire is hot.

Will the dog get a hotdog?

Ann tosses the dog a hotdog.

Two Syllables

1. Flash card practice:

   Ă, Ĕ, Ĭ, Ŏ, Ŭ, Ô, Ō, Ī,
   ST, W, P, SM

2. **_Point_** at the new word and say, "This word has two syllables. The first syllable is a word we learned in Book 1."

3. Sound out the new word.

4. Read the story.

5. **_Point_** at "tosses" and ask:

"What is the root word in 'tosses?'" (toss)

"What is the suffix?" (es)

6. Say "tosses" slowly and ask: "Can you hear the two syllables?"

7. **_Ask:_** "How many syllables does 'hotdog' have?" Be sure to say the word slowly, emphasizing the two syllables.

tôss|ĕs

Writing Practice

small   small small

bone   bone bone

bones   bones bones

home   home home

fire   fire fire

log   log log

hot   hot hot

A hot fire.   A hot fire.

Ann has hotdogs.

Ann has hotdogs.

Learn to Read with REAL Phonics, Book 2
By Kallie Woods
© 2012 Broden Books, LLC., Minneapolis, Mn. USA

Download this handwriting worksheet at:
BrodenBooks.com

The Kite

This man sells kites.

The man sells Ann a big kite.

Ann runs fast.

Ann goes up the hill.

Learning to Read - The Letter K

1. **_Point_** at the kite and explain that K has the "kk" sound, as in "kite."

2. **_Point_** at the first new word and ask, "Is the I long or short?" (Long)

3. **_Ask:_** "Why is the I long?"

(Because of the silent E)

4. **_Ask:_** "What does long I sound like?"

(Like "eye" as in "ice cream")

5. Sound out the new words and read the story.

6. Get out your flash cards for K and C and explain that these two letters have the same sound.

kīte
kītes

K k

On the Hill Top

Ann goes to the top of the hill.

Ann runs and runs.

Will the kite go up?

It goes up fast!

New Word

1. Practice with the letter side of the following flash cards:

    Ă, Ĕ, Ĭ, Ŏ, Ŭ, Ô, Ō, Ī,
    ST, W, P, SM, K,
    to, the, of

2. **_Point_** at the word "goes" in the last panel and ask: "What is the rule for two vowels together?

(The first one is usually long, the second one is silent)

3. Sound out the new word and read the story.

4. **_Ask:_** "How do you spell

    'to?'" (T-O)
    'of?'" (O-F)

tŏp

The Ant Has a Kite

That ant has a small kite.

The ant goes up to the fan.

Dan has his hand on the fan.

The fan is on!

Review

1. Find the exclamation point in the story.

2. *__Ask__:* "What does an exclamation point mean?"

    (Surprise or excitement)

3. Read the story together with emphasis on the exclamation point.

4. *__Point__* at the word "goes" in the second panel and ask, "What is the rule when two vowels are together?"

    (The first one is usually long, the second one is silent)

The Ant Lands at Home

The kite goes up.

The ant goes up.

The kite lands on top of the anthill.

The ant is home.

New Words with Short A

1. Sound out the first two new words.

2. **_Point_** at the last new word and say: "Here is another compound word. It's made of two smaller words put together."

3. Sound out the last new word and read the story.

4. **_Ask:_** "How many syllables does 'land' have?" (one)

5. **_Ask:_** "How many syllables does 'anthill' have?" (two)

lănd
lănds
ănt | hĭll

Drop the Ball

The dog has a ball.

The dog drops the ball at the fire.

The fire is hot.

The ball gets hot.

Learning to Read Words With DR

1. Practice with the letter side of these flash cards:

   Ă, Ĕ, Ĭ, Ŏ, Ŭ, Ô, Ō, Ī,
   ST, W, P, SM, K

2. **_Ask:_** "What are the 5 vowels?"

   (A, E, I, O, U)

3. **_Point_** at the DR panel and ask, "Are the letters D and R vowels or consonants?" (Consonants)

4. Explain that D and R together have the "drr" sound, as in "drop."

5. Sound out the new words and read the story.

Dr
dr

drŏp, drŏps

A Hot Ball

Dan bats the hot ball.

That rat has the ball.

Will the rat drop the ball?

The rat drops the hot ball.

Review Suffixes and Root Words

1. Read the story.

2. **_Point_** at the word "bats" and ask, "What is the suffix on the end of this word?"

   (s)

3. **_Ask:_** "What is the root word?" (bat)

4. **_Point_** at the word "drops" and ask, "What is the suffix on the end of this word?"

   (s)

5. **_Ask:_** "What is the root word?"

   (drop)

st	<u>fast</u>, stab, stand, stamp stem, step, stiff, still, stop stub, stuff, stump store, stone, stole
dr	dress, drum, drug <u>drop</u>, <u>drops</u>, drip, drips
sm	<u>small</u>, smell, smells smile, smiles, smoke
P, p	<u>past</u>, pan, pat, pad, pant, pants pig, pit, pin, pet, pen pot, pop pipe, pine, pane, pole, pile, poke
K, k	kid, kiss, kit, kill <u>kite</u>
W, w	<u>will</u>, wall, wet, went win, wind, with wire, wipe, wide, wife, woke

Practice New Letter Sounds

1. Explain that this page has some old words and some new words. The words we already know are underlined.

2. Sound out the practice words, defining any unfamiliar words as you go.

3. Note: The point of this page is not to learn new words, but to become more familiar with the new letter sounds in the left column. Give as much help as is needed.

Ann Rides A Bike

This is Ann's bike.

Can Ann ride the bike?

Ann rides up the hill.

The bike goes fast on the hill.

Words With Long I, Silent E

1. **_Point_** at the first new word and ask, "What letter is silent in this new word?"

    (Silent E)

2. **_Ask:_** "What does the silent E do to the I?"

    (It makes it long)

3. **_Ask:_** "What does long I sound like?" ("Eye" as in "ice cream")

4. Sound out the new words and read the story.

5. **_Point_** at "rides" and ask, "What is the root word?" (ride)

6. **_Ask:_** "What is the suffix?" (s)

bīke
rīde
rīdes

Ann's Kite

The kite goes up.

Ann rides the bike past Dan.

Ann goes past the dog.

Ann rides the bike home.

Review

1. **_Ask:_** "What are the 5 vowels?" (A, E, I, O, U)

2. **_Point_** at the word "goes" and ask: "What is the rule for two vowels together?"

    (The first one is usually long, the second one is silent)

3. **_Ask:_** "What letter has to be in every word?"

    (A vowel)

4. Read the story.

Writing Practice

kite   kite   kite

drop   drop   drop

drops   drops   drops

bike   bike   bike

ride   ride   ride

rides   rides   rides

Ann rides a bike.

Ann rides a bike.

That ant has a kite.

That ant has a kite.

Learn to Read with REAL Phonics, Book 2
By Kallie Woods
© 2012 Broden Books, LLC., Minneapolis, Mn. USA

The Cat in the Log

This fire got the cat hot.

The cat got off the log.

The cat goes in the log.

That dog runs at the cat.

Review Suffixes and Root Words

1. Read the story.

2. ***Point*** at the word "runs" and ask, "What is the suffix on this word?"

    (s)

3. ***Ask:*** "What is the root word?" (run)

A Bad Sad Dog

The dog goes in the log.

Dan tugs on the dog.

Bad dog!

The dog is sad.

New Words with Short A

1. **_Point_** at the new words and ask: "What are the vowels in the new words?" (Short A)

2. Sound out the new words.

3. **_Ask:_** "What does an exclamation point mean?" (Surprise or excitement)

4. Find the exclamation point and read the story.

bǎd, sǎd

Hot and Cold

Ann is cold.

Dan fans the fire.

The fire gets big.

Lots of logs go in the fire.

Long O Followed By L

1. ***Point*** at the new word and explain that when O is followed by L, the O can be long or short.

2. ***Ask:*** "What is the vowel in the new word?"

   (Long O)

3. Sound out the new word and read the story.

cōld

A Cold Cat

The cat is cold.

The fire is hot.

The cat sits at the fire.

The cat is not cold.

Review

1. ***Ask:*** "How do you spell

   'to?' "
   'of?' "
   'the?' "

2. ***If you skipped Book 1 ask:***
"What are the 5 vowels?"

   (A, E, I, O, U)

3. ***If you skipped Book 1 ask:***
"What letter has to be in every
word?" (A vowel)

4. ***If you skipped Book 1 ask:***
"What is a consonant?"

   (Any letter that's not a
vowel)

5. Read the story.

6. ***Point*** at the word "cold" in
the 4th panel, and ask, "What
happens when O is followed
by L?"

   (The O can be long or
short)

Rocks on the Dock

Dan goes on the dock.

A rock is in his hand.

Can Dan hit the log?

The rock lands on the log!

The CK Sound

1. Get out your flash cards for C, K and CK. Explain that C, K and CK all have the same sound.

2. Sound out the new words together, find all the CK's in the story, then read the story.

3. **_Point_** at the new words and ask: "Which one of the new words has a suffix?" (rocks)

4. **_Ask:_** "What is the suffix?" (s)

ck

dŏck
rŏck
rŏcks

A Sack of Rocks

Dan has a small sack of rocks on the dock.

Dan tosses a rock at the log.

The rock drops on top of the log.

Dan tosses them all at the log.

Learning to Read - Another CK Word

1. ***Point*** at the new word and ask: "What does CK on the end of a word sound like?"

2. Sound out the new word and read the story.

3. Read the next page together, then let your student trace the words.

săck

Writing Practice

bad   bad   bad

sad   sad   sad

cold   cold   cold

sack   sack   sack

dock   dock   dock

rock   rock   rock

Dan has a rock.

Dan has a rock.

Can Dan hit the log?

Can Dan hit the log?

Learn to Read with REAL Phonics, Book 2
By Kallie Woods
© 2012 Broden Books, LLC., Minneapolis, Mn. USA

Download this page free at:
www.BrodenBooks.com

Back at the Dock

Dan goes back home to get his cat.

Dan goes back to the dock.

The cat has a big sack of rocks on his back.

Can the cat toss a rock on the log?

Learning to Read - Another CK Word

1. **_Point_** at the new word and ask: "What does CK on the end of a word sound like?"

2. Sound out the new word.

3. Find all the words in the story with CK.

4. Read the story.

bǎck

The Cat and the Rocks

The cat's hand is in the sack.

The cat can not toss a rock on the log.

The cat hands Dan a rock.

Dan's rock lands on the log.

Review & Phonics Flash Cards

1. Practice with your flash cards for the following letters. Show the letter side first, and ask for the letter sound. Do not show the picture side unless your student needs a hint.

   Ă, Ě, Ĭ, Ŏ, Ŭ, Ô, Ō, Ī,
   ST, W, P, SM, K, DR, CK

2. Read the story.

3. **_Point_** at "cat's" and ask: "What does apostrophe-S mean?"

   (Something belongs to someone)

4. **_Ask:_** "What belongs to the cat?" (His hand)

The Log Home

This is a log.

This fat rat has his home in the log.

His log is up on top of a hill.

The rat is cold in his log home.

Easy Spelling Words

1. **_Ask:_** "How do you spell ...

    'to?'"
    'of?'"
    'the?'"
    'is?'"
    'on?'"

2. Read the story.

3. **_Point_** at the word "cold" and ask, "What happens when O is followed by L?"

(The O can be long or short)

A Wet Rat

The fat rat got up on the log.

The log is wet.

The rat falls off of the wet log.

The rat lands in the mud. The mud is wet and cold.

New Word with Short E

1. **_Ask:_** "What is the vowel in the new word?"

   (Short E)

2. Sound out the new word.

3. Read the story.

4. **_Point_** at the word "cold" in the 4th panel and ask, "What happens when O is followed by an L?"

   (The O can be long or short)

wĕt

The Tire on the Hill

That man has a lot of tires.

Bella gets a tire.

Bella gets in the tire.

The tire goes fast on the hill.

More Long I, Silent E

1. ***Point*** at the new words and ask: "What letter is silent in the new words?" (Silent E)

2. ***Ask:*** "What does Silent E do to the other vowel?"

    (It makes it long)

3. Sound out the new words.

4. Read the story.

5. ***Point*** at the new words and ask: "Which word has a suffix?"

    (tires)

6. ***Ask:*** "What is the suffix?" (s)

tīrҽ
tīrҽs

Bella Goes Off the Dock

The tire goes past Matt.

It goes on the dock.

The tire falls off of the dock.

Bella gets wet. It is cold.

Easy Spelling Words

1. Flash cards: to, of, the

2. Read the story.

3. Note: This page presents a good opportunity for spelling practice with the words "off" and "of," as they appear side-by-side in the story.

4. *Ask:* "How do you spell 'of?'" Hold up the flash card if necessary.

5. *Ask:* "How do you spell 'off?'" Point at the word in the third panel if necessary.

The Old Man's Cats

This old man has big cats,

and small cats,

and fat cats,

and tall cats.

A Rhyming Story

1. ***Point*** at the new word and ask: "What happens when O is followed by L?"

   (The O can be long or short)

2. ***Ask:*** "What does the straight line mean over the O?"

   (It means the O is long)

3. Sound out the new word.

4. ***Ask:*** "What do commas mean?"

   (They mean you should pause)

5. Find the commas in the story.

6. ***Ask:*** "What do sentences end with?" (A period)

7. Find the period and explain that this story has one long sentence.

8. Read the story.

ōld

All the Cats

The old cats sit,

the fast cats run,

the bad cat bit the sad cat,

and the small cat sat in the sun.

Poetry for Beginning Readers

1. **_Ask:_** "What is the vowel in the new word?" (Short U)

2. Sound out the new word.

3. Explain that this story is a poem with one long sentence, and three commas.

4. Find the commas.

5. Read the story.

6. After your student has read the story, read it back to him or her with emphasis on the rhyming words.

sŭn

Matt's Old Tire

Matt has an old tire.

Matt rolled the tire.

Can Matt roll the tire up the hill?

Matt rolled the tire to the top of the hill.

Learning to Read - Words with Long O

1. ***Point*** at the new words and ask: "What happens when O is followed by L?"

(The O can be long or short)

2. Sound out the new words.

3. ***Point*** at "rolled" and ask:

"What is the root word?"

(roll)

"What is the suffix?"

(ed)

4. Read the story.

rōll
rōlléd

Matt Rolled and Fell

Matt got in the tire.

The tire rolled fast on the hill.

The tire hit a rock.

Matt fell in the mud.

New Word with Short E

1. **_Ask:_** "What is the vowel in the new word?"

   (Short E)

2. Sound out the new word and find it in the story.

3. Read the story.

4. **_Point_** at the second panel and ask, "Which word in this panel has a suffix?" (rolled)

fĕll

Writing Practice

back   back back

wet   wet wet

tire   tire tire

tires   tires tires

old   old old

roll   roll roll

rolled   rolled rolled

fell   fell fell

The cat sat in the sun.

The cat sat in the sun.

Learn to Read with REAL Phonics, Book 2
By Kallie Woods
© 2012 Broden Books, LLC., Minneapolis, Mn. USA

The Cat Rolls

The cat gets in the small tire.

The tire rolls on the hill.

The tire rolls on the ant.

The ant fell on his back.

New Word with Long O

1. ***Point*** at the new word and ask:

"What happens when O is followed by L?"

   (The O can be long or short)

"What is the vowel in this word?" (Long O)

2. Sound out the new word and read the story.

rōlls

The Tire Hits a Rock

The tire rolled on the hill.

It hit a rock.

The cat got up,

and the cat fell back.

Review Punctuation

1. **_Ask_:** "What does a comma mean?"

   (You should pause)

2. Find the comma in the story.

3. **_Ask_:** "What does every sentence end with?"

   (A period)

4. **_Ask_:** "How many sentences are in this story?"

   (Three)

5. Read the story.

6. **_Point_** at the word "rolled" and ask:

   "What is the root word"?   (roll)

   "What is the suffix?"   (ed)

A Big Kick

The rat is in his log on top of the hill.

Dan kicks the log.

The log rolls on the hill.

The log rolls fast.

Learning to Read - CK and K

1. **_Point_** at the first new word and ask, "What does CK sound like?"

2. **_Ask:_** "What two parts of this word have the same sound?"

    (The K and the CK)

3. Sound out the new words.

4. **_Point_** at "kicks" and ask:

"What is the suffix on 'kicks?'" (s)

"What is the root word?" (kick)

5. Read the story.

kĭck
kĭcks

A Rat in the Mud

The log rolled past Ann.

It rolled past the cat.

It went in the mud.

The rat is mad!

New Word With Short E

1. Practice with your alphabet flash cards for the following letters:

   Ă, Ĕ, Ĭ, Ŏ, Ŭ, Ô, Ō, Ī,
   ST, W, P, SM, K, DR, CK

2. *Ask:* "What is the vowel in the new word?"

   (Short E)

3. Sound out the new word.

4. Read the story.

wĕnt

A Cat in the Bed

Dan had a bad cold.

Dan went to bed.

Will Dan let the cat up in bed?

Dan lets the cat in bed.

Words with Short Vowels

1. **_Ask:_** "What are vowels in the new words?"

   (Short E and Short A)

2. Sound out the new words.

3. **_Point_** at the new words and ask: "Which word has a suffix?" (lets)

4. **_Ask:_** "What is the suffix on the word 'lets?'"

   (s)

5. Read the story.

lĕt

lĕts

bĕd

hăd

A Sad Cat

The cat went to bed with Dan.

Dan kicked and rolled.

The cat fell off of the bed.

The cat is sad.

Learning to Read - Words with Short I

1. Cover up the "ed" in "kicked," and say, "This is a word we've had before."

2. Sound out the new words.

3. ***Point*** at "kicked" and ask: "What is the suffix on "kicked?" (ed)

4. Read the story.

5. ***Ask:*** "How do you spell ...

   'of?'"
   'off?'"
   'to?'"
   'the?'"

kĭckĕd
wĭth

The Cat Bed

A man had cat beds to sell.

The man had big beds and small beds.

The man had lots of cat beds.

Dan got his cat a small bed.

Review

1. Read the story.

2. ***Ask:*** "What size cat bed did Dan get?"

   (A small bed)

Note: Comprehension questions train your child to pay attention to what he is reading.

The Cat Has A Nap

Dan went home with the bed.

Will the cat get in the bed?

The cat had a nap in the bed.

Dan had a nap in his bed.

New Word with Short A

1. Practice with your flash cards for the following letters:

   Ă, Ĕ, Ĭ, Ŏ, Ŭ, Ô, Ō, Ī, N, P

2. Sound out the new word.

3. Read the story.

4. *Ask:* "What letter has to be in every word?"

   (A vowel)

5. Read the next page together before beginning the writing practice.

năp

Writing Practice

went went went

with with with

kick kick kick

kicked kicked kicked

let let let

lets lets lets

Dan had a nap in bed.

The cat had a nap.

Dan kicks the log.

Dan kicks the log.

The Shells

This is Ann's shop.

The shop has shells to sell.

The shop has big shells and small shells.

Ann has lots of shells.

Learning to Read - Words with SH

1. *Point* at the ship and ask: "Are S and H vowels or consonants?"

(Consonants)

2. Explain that SH has the "shhh" sound, as in "ship." Say the "shhh" sound together.

3. *Ask:* "What are the vowels in the new words?"

(Short O and Short E)

4. Sound out the new words and read the story.

shŏp
shĕll
shĕlls

Sh, sh

Ann Sells the Shells

Ann sold Dan a shell.

Ann sold a man a shell.

Ann sold all the shells,

then Ann went back home.

New Words

1. ***Point*** at the first new word and ask: "What happens when O is followed by L?"

(The O can be long or short)

2. ***Ask***: "What are the vowels in the new words?"

(Long O, Short E)

3. Sound out the new words, find the comma and read the story.

sōld
thĕn

She Sells Balls

Ann went to the shop.

She had lots of balls to sell.

She sold a ball to Dan.

He kicked the ball.

Learning to Read - Long E

1. ***Point*** at the eagle and say, "Long E sounds like 'ee' as in 'eagle.'"

2. Go to page 8 and teach the long E section.

3. ***Point*** at the new words and ask: "Is a vowel long or short on the end of a word?"

(long)

4. Sound out the new words "she" and "he."

5. Explain that the E on the end of "she" and "he" is not silent because it is the only vowel in the word, and every word has to have at least one

vowel that you can hear.

6. Read the story.

shē, hē

Ē, ē

He Kicks the Ball

Dan kicked the ball.

It rolled to the dog.

The dog got the ball,

then he ran to Dan.

Review

1. Practice with your alphabet flash cards for the following letters. Show the letter side first, and ask for the letter sound. Do not show the picture side unless your student needs a hint.

Ă, Ĕ, Ĭ, Ŏ, Ŭ, Ô, Ō, Ī, Ē
ST, W, P, SM, K, DR, CK, SH

2. _**Ask**_: "What does a comma mean?"

(It means you should pause)

3. Find the comma.

4. Read the story.

5. _**Ask**_: "How many sentences does the story have?" (three)

Ann Likes to Sell Bikes

Ann went to the shop.

She had bikes to sell.

Dan got a small bike.

Will he like his bike?

Learning to Read - Words with Long I

1. ***Point*** at the first new word and ask: "What vowels are in this new word?"

    (Long I and Silent E)

2. ***Ask:*** "Why is the I long?"

    (Because of the Silent E)

3. Sound out the new words and read the story.

4. ***Point*** at the new words and ask: "Which word has a suffix?"

    (likes)

līke līkes

Dan Likes His Bike

Dan got on the bike.

He went on the hill.

The bike went fast.

Dan likes the bike a lot!

Review

1. *__Ask:__* "How do you spell 'the?'" (T-H-E)

2. *__Ask:__* "How do you spell 'on?'" (O-N)

3. Read the story

The Bike Ride

Dan jumps on his bike.

He rides past Ann's shop.

He rides to the dock.

He jumps off the bike.

The Letter J

1. **_Point_** at the jelly and explain that J has the "juh" sound, as in "jelly."

2. **_Ask:_** "What vowel is in the new words?"

   (Short U)

3. Sound out the new words and read the story.

4. **_Point_** at the new words and ask: "Which word has a suffix?"

   (jumps)

jŭmp
jŭmps

J j

Writing Practice

shell   shell   shell

she   she   she

he   he   he

like   like   like

likes   likes   likes

jumps   jumps   jumps

Dan likes to jump.

Dan likes to jump.

Ann sells a shell.

Ann sells a shell.

Learn to Read with REAL Phonics, Book 2
By Kallie Woods
© 2012 Broden Books, LLC., Minneapolis, Mn. USA

Download this page free at:
www.BrodenBooks.com

Dan Jumps In

Dan went to the end of the dock.

Will he jump in?

He jumps in.

Dan likes to get wet.

New Word with Short E

1. Practice with your flash cards for the following letters. Show the letter side first and ask for the letter sound. Don't show the picture side unless your student needs a hint.

Ă, Ě, Ĭ, Ŏ, Ŭ, Ô, Ō, Ī, Ē
ST, W, P, SM, K, DR, CK, SH, J

2. *Ask*: "What vowel is in the new word?"

(Short E)

3. Sound out the new word and read the story.

ĕnd

Tie the Rope

Ann has a rope to tie the dog.

She ties the end of the rope to the dog.

The dog likes to run.

The rope is in Ann's hand.

New Words with Silent E

1. ***Point*** at the first new word and ask: "What is the rule for two vowels together?"

(The first one is usually long, the second one is silent)

2. Sound out the new words and read the story.

3. ***Point*** at the word "Ann's" and ask: "What does apostrophe-S mean?"

(Something belongs to someone)

4. ***Ask:*** "What belongs to Ann?"

(Ann's hand)

tīe
tīes
rōpe

A Nap in Ann's Lap

Ann tied up the dog.

She had a nap.

The dog got in Ann's lap.

The dog had a nap with Ann.

New Words

1. ***Point*** at the first new word and ask: "What is the rule for two vowels together?"

   (The first one is usually long, the second one is silent)

2. Sound out the new words.

3. Read the story.

tīed
lăp

Bella Sees An Anthill

Bella sees an ant.

The ant goes in the anthill.

Bella can see a small hole in the anthill.

The ants all go in the hole.

New Words with Two Vowels Together

1. Review the page 8 "E" section.

2. **_Point_** at the first two new words and ask: "What is the rule for two vowels that appear together?"

   (The first one is usually long, the second one is silent)

3. Sound out the first two new words.

4. **_Point_** at the last two new words and ask: "What vowels are in these two new words?"

   (Long O and Silent E)

5. Sound out the last two new words and read the story.

sēe̸

sēe̸s

hōle̸

hōle̸s

Dig, Dig, Dig!

This dog likes to dig.

He dug a big hole.

He went in the hole.

See all the holes he has dug!

Review Easy Spelling Words

1. Read the story.

2. ***Ask:*** "How do you spell ...

    'to?'"
    'of?'"
    'the?'"

Sweep It Up!

The dog digs up a lot of mud.

The old man sees the mud.

He has to sweep up all the mud.

He sweeps and sweeps and sweeps.

The SW Sound

1. ***Point*** at the swan and explain that the consonants S and W make the "sw" sound, as in "swan."

2. ***Point*** at the new words and ask, "What is the rule for two vowels together?"

   (The first one is usually long and the second one is silent)

3. Sound out the new words and ask, "Which new word has a suffix?"

   (sweeps)

4. Read the story.

Sw, sw

swēep swēeps

77

Writing Practice

rope   rope   rope

tie   tie   tie

ties   ties   ties

lap   lap   lap

hole   hole   hole

holes   holes   holes

sweep   sweep   sweep

see   see   see

Ann sees a shell.

Ann sees a shell.

Learn to Read with REAL Phonics, Book 2
By Kallie Woods
© 2012 Broden Books, LLC., Minneapolis, Mn. USA

Download free handwriting worksheets at:
www.BrodenBooks.com

The Rope Swing

Matt had a rope.

He went up the tree,

then he tied the rope to the tree.

This is Matt's rope swing.

The ING Sound

1. ***Point*** at the ring and explain that the letters "I-N-G" sound like "ing" as in "ring."

2. Sound out the new words.

3. Read the story.

swĭng
swĭngs

ĭng

Matt Goes Swimming

Matt swings on the rope.

He jumps off.

Can he swim?

He swims to the dock.

New Words with the SW Sound

1. Practice with your flash cards for the following letters:

Ă, Ĕ, Ĭ, Ŏ, Ŭ, Ô, Ē, Ō, Ī, M, ST, W, P, SM, K, DR, CK, SH, J, SW, ING

2. *__Point__* at the first new word and ask, "How many syllables does this word have?" (2)

3. Explain that each syllable has it's own vowel.

4. Sound out the new words and read the story.

5. *__Point__* at "swimming" and ask:

"What is the suffix?" (ing)
"What is the root word?" (swim)

swĭm | mĭng
swĭm
swĭms

Bella Swings on the Rope

Ann sees Matt swimming.

Then she sees Bella get hold of the rope.

Bella holds the rope and swings.

She lets go and jumps off.

Learning to Read - Words with Long O

1. ***Point*** at the new words and ask, "What happens when O is followed by L?"

   (The O can be long or short)

2. Sound out the new words.

3. ***Ask:*** "Which new word has a suffix?"

   (holds)

4. ***Ask:*** "What is the suffix?" (s)

5. ***Ask:*** "What is the root word?" (hold)

6. Read the story.

hōld, hōlds

Ann Goes Swimming

Ann has a hold of the rope.

Ann's feet go in the rope and she swings.

She lets go of the rope and jumps off.

Ann and Bella swim back to the dock.

Learning to Read - Words with Double E

1. *Ask:* "What is the rule when two vowels are together?"

   (The first one is long and the second one is silent)

2. Sound out the new word.

3. Read the story.

fēet

A Bee in the Tree

That is a bee.

The cat sees the bee.

The bee goes in the hole in the tree.

The cat jumps on the tree.

More Double E Words

1. **_Ask:_** "What is the rule when two vowels are together?"

   (The first one is usually long and the second one is silent)

2. Sound out the new words.

3. Read the story.

bē̶e̶

bē̶e̶s̶

trē̶e̶

Tr
tr

Writing Practice

swing   swing   swing

swim   swim   swim

swimming   swimming

hold   hold   hold

holds   holds   holds

feet   feet   feet

bee   bee   bee

bees   bees   bees

A cat goes up the tree.

A cat goes up the tree.

Learn to Read with REAL Phonics, Book 2
By Kallie Woods
© 2012 Broden Books, LLC., Minneapolis, Mn. USA

Download this page free at:
www.BrodenBooks.com

Bees in the Tree

The cat sees the bees in the tree hole.

The cat is hitting the hole.

The bees get mad and they bite the cat.

The cat jumps off the tree and runs home.

New Sight Word - "They"

1. Sound out the first new word.

2. ***Point*** at the second new word and ask: "How many syllables do you see?" (two)

3. Sound out the second new word.

4. ***Point*** to the third new word and explain that it is the sight word "they." It starts with TH like "thumb" and "the," but we will not sound it out.

5. Find the word "they" in the story.

6. Read the story.

A Bite to Eat

Dan's cat needs to eat.

He goes to Dan.

They sit and rock.

Will he get a bite to eat?

New Words With Double Vowels

1. ***Point*** at the new words and ask: "What is the rule for two vowels together?"

    (The first one is usually long and the second one is silent)

2. Sound out the new words and read the story.

3. ***Point*** at the new words and ask, "Which of these new words has a suffix?" (needs)

4. Practice with the following flash cards:

    they, of, to, the

ēat
nēed
nēeds

Feed the Cat

Dan feeds his cat.

The cat eats a lot.

He needs to sleep it off.

He jumps in bed and goes to sleep.

The SL Sound

1. **_Point_** at the sled and explain that S and L have the "slll" sound together.

2. **_Point_** at the new words and ask, "Which vowel is silent when two vowels are together?" (The second one is silent)

3. **_Ask:_** "What does the silent vowel do to the other vowel?"

(It makes it long)

4. Sound out the new words.

slēep, ēats
fēed, fēeds

Sl
sl

sw	<u>swim</u>, <u>swing</u>, swam <u>swell</u>, swift <u>sweep</u>, swipe, sweet
ĭng	<u>hitting</u>, <u>swing</u>, <u>swimming</u>, ring, sing sting, thing, king, wing
sh	<u>she</u>, <u>shell</u>, shed, ship <u>shop</u>, shot, shut share, shake, shape, shine, sheet
ck	<u>back</u>, <u>sack</u>, rack, stack, shack neck, deck, peck, pick, nick, lick <u>rock</u>, <u>dock</u>, sock, lock, sick, tick luck, duck, buck, tuck
ēe̸	<u>bee</u>, beef, deep, deer, teen <u>feed</u>, <u>need</u>, seed, weed, beep, keep <u>feet</u>, weep, week, sheep, street
___e̸	pine, fine, line, mine, nine, wine, shine <u>bone</u>, <u>hole</u>, <u>rope</u>, <u>home</u>, nose, rose, poke <u>ride</u>, <u>bike</u>, <u>like</u>, <u>kite</u>, <u>fire</u>, <u>tire</u>

Practice New Letter Sounds

1. **_Explain:_** "This page has some old words and some new words. The words that you already know are underlined."

2. Sound out all the words, starting at the top.

3. When you get to the EE row ask: "What is the rule when two vowels are together?"

(The first one is usually long, the second one is silent)

4. When you get to the last row ask: "What does Silent E sound like?" (Nothing! It's silent!)

5. **_Ask:_** "What does Silent E do to the other vowel in the word?" (It makes it long)

Bella Rides Her Bike

Bella got on her bike.

She feels like going fast.

She goes up the hill.

She likes going fast on the hill.

New Sight Word

1. ***Point*** at the first new word and say: "This is the sight word 'her.' We are not going to sound it out. Can you find it in the story?"

2. ***Point*** at the second new word and ask: "How many syllables does this word have?" (two)

3. Explain that the first syllable is a word we know and the second syllable is a suffix we know.

4. Sound out the remaining new words and read the story.

her

gō|ĭng, fēel, fēels

Jumping is Fun

Bella sees a pothole, but she cannot stop her bike.

The bike goes up!

She jumps the pothole.

Bella likes to jump with her bike.

Compound Words

1. Sound out the first two new words.

2. **_Point_** at the last two new words and explain that they are compound words. Compound words are made up of two smaller words put together.

3. Sound out the last two new words.

4. **_Flash Cards_:** they, her, of, to, the

5. **_Ask_:** "What does a comma mean?"

   (It means you should pause)

6. Find the comma, then read the story.

stŏp
jŭmp|ĭng
pŏt|hōle
căn|nŏt

Writing Practice

feel

hitting

cannot

needs

sleep

He is going to feed her.

They will stop jumping.

Eat a bite.

Learn to Read with REAL Phonics
By Kallie Woods
© 2012 Broden Books, LLC., Minneapolis, Mn. USA

The Junk In the Dump

Matt had a sack of junk.

He dropped his sack in the dump.

The dump had lots of old junk.

Matt sees an old tire.

New Words

1. **_Ask:_** "What vowel is in the first two new words?"

   (Short U)

2. Sound out the first two new words.

3. **_Ask:_** "What vowels are in the third new word?"

   (Short O and Silent E)

4. Sound out the third new word and read the story.

5. Flash cards:

   they, her, the, of, to

dŭmp
jŭnk
drŏppéd

The Tire Swing

Matt is rolling his tire to the tree.

He ties the tire on the rope.

He gets on the tire.

He swings on the rope.

New Word with Two Syllables

1. ***Point*** at the new word and ask: "What happens when O is followed by L?"

   (The O can be long or short)

2. ***Ask:*** "What are the vowels in this word?"

   (Long O, Short I)

3. ***Ask:*** "How many syllables does this word have?"

   (two)

4. ***Ask:*** "What is the suffix on this word?" (ing)

5. Sound out the new word and read the story.

rōll|ĭng

Running With Dan

Dan went running.

The dog went with him.

They went past the dock.

They went up the hill.

Learning to Read - Words with Short Vowels

1. Flash cards:

    they, her, the, of, to

2. Sound out the new words.

3. ***Point*** at the last new word and ask: "What is the suffix on this word?" (I-N-G)

4. ***Ask:*** "How many syllables does 'running' have?" (two)

5. Read the story.

hĭm
rŭn|nĭng

Running And Jumping

Dan sees the big pothole.

He is going to jump.

Dan is jumping the pothole.

The dog jumps with him.

Review Compound Words

1. **_Ask:_** "What is a compound word?"

   (Two words put together)

2. **_Point_** at the words "pothole" and "jumping" and ask: "Which one of these words is a compound word?" (pothole)

3. **_Ask:_** "What are the two smaller words in 'pothole?'"

   ("pot" and "hole")

4. Read the story.

A Bus Ride to the Store

Ann likes going to the store to shop.

She went to the bus stop.

She got on her bus.

Her bus went up the hill.

The OR Sound

1. **_Point_** at the orange and say: "The letters O and R together sound like 'or' as in 'orange.'" Say the "or" sound together.

2. **_Ask:_** "What do the letters S and T sound like together?"

   (Like "sst" as in "star")

3. Sound out the new words.

4. Find OR in the story.

5. Read the story.

Or, or

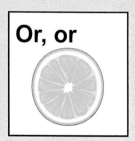

stōre bŭs

96

Shopping For A Dog Bed

Ann jumps off the bus at the pet store.

She is shopping for a dog bed.

Ann rides the bus home with the dog bed in her lap.

She jumps off the bus at home.

Double Consonants with ING

1. Cover the F in "for" and ask, "What does O-R sound like?"

2. Sound out the first two words.

3. **_Point_** to the third new word and ask: "How many syllables does this word have?" (two)

4. Sound out the 3rd new word and read the story.

5. **_Explain:_** Whenever you want to add ING to a word, you double the last consonant, then add ING.

6. **_Ask:_** "What is the last consonant in the word 'shop?'" (P)

7. Find the double consonant words ending with ING on pages 80, 85 and 94.

fōr
pĕt
shŏp|pĭng

A Sack of Seeds

Ann went shopping for a sack of seeds at the store.

She dug a lot of holes.

She dropped in the seeds.

Then she got her seeds wet.

Learning to Read Words with Long E

1. **_Ask:_** "What is the rule for two vowels together?"

   (The first one is usually long, the second one is silent)

2. Sound out the new words.

3. Read the story.

4. **_Point_** at "seeds" and ask,

"What is the root word?"

   (seed)

"What is the suffix?"

   (s)

sēed

sēeds

Writing Practice

dump

junk

seed

for

store

shopping

running

rolling

His pet went with him.

Learn to Read with REAL Phonics
By Kallie Woods
© 2012 Broden Books, LLC., Minneapolis, Mn. USA

Weed Seeds and Bees

Ann went to see the seeds.

She sees lots of weeds.

The bees like the weeds.

She digs up the weeds.

New Words Beginning with W

1. **_Ask:_** "What is the rule for two vowels together?"

   (The first one is usually long, the second one is silent)

2. Sound out the new words.

3. Read the story.

4. **_Point_** at "weeds" and ask: "What is the root word?"

   (weed)

   "What is the suffix?"

   (s)

wēed

wēeds

Picking A Ball

Ann is going to her shop.

She has a lot of balls to sell.

A small man needs to pick a ball.

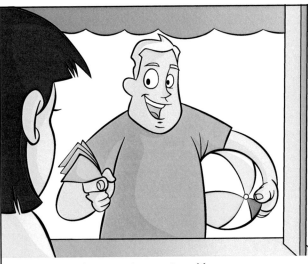

He picks a big ball.

More CK Words

1. Sound out the new words.

2. ***Point*** at "picking" and ask:

"What is the root word" (pick)

"What is the suffix?" (ing)

"How many syllables does 'picking' have?" (two)

3. Explain that we don't have to double the consonant in "picking," because it's already doubled. CK is a double consonant. "Double" just means two of something.

4. ***Ask:*** "What would a double ice cream cone look like?"

(Two scoops of ice cream)

pĭck
pĭcks
pĭck|ĭng

Balls Needed

The tall man picked up a ball.

He needed a lot of balls,

so Ann sold him all the balls,

and then she went home.

New Words with Mixed Vowels

1. *Ask:* "What are the vowels in the first new word?"

   (Short I and Silent E)

2. *Ask:* "What are the vowels in the second new word?"

   (Long E, Silent E, Short E)

3. Sound out the new words.

4. *Ask:* "Which new word has two syllables?" (needed)

5. *Ask:* "How many sentences are in this story?" (two)

6. Read the story.

pĭckĕd
nēĕd|ĕd

Shopping For Roses

Ann and Bella rode to the store.

Bella sees a rose in the store.

They got a lot of roses,

Then they tied the roses to the bikes.

Four New Words

1. *Flash cards:*

   they, her, to, of, the

2. Sound out the new words.

3. *Ask:* "How many syllables does 'roses' have?" (two)

4. Find the comma in the story.

5. Read the story.

bīkes
rōde
rōse
rōs|ĕs

Weeds and Roses

Ann and Bella pick all the weeds.

Bella is digging holes for the roses.

Ann is dropping the roses in the holes.

She is getting the roses wet.

New Words Ending With ING

1. Cover the second syllables in the three new words, then sound out the first syllables.

2. *__Point__* at "getting" and ask, "How do we change 'get' to 'getting?'"

(Double the T and add ING)

3. *__Point__* at "digging" and ask, "How do we change 'dig' to 'digging?'"

(Double the G and add ING)

4. *__Point__* at "dropping" and repeat the above question.

5. Read the story.

gĕt | tĭng
dĭg | gĭng
drŏp | pĭng

Bees in the Roses

Ann and Bella went to see the roses.

They see a lot of bees.

A big fat bee buzzes in the roses.

The bees all buzz a lot.

The Letter Z

1. ***Point*** at the zebra and explain that the letter Z sounds like "zz" as in "zebra."

2. Sound out the new words and read the story.

3. Get out your flash cards for S and Z. Explain that S has a soft "sss" sound, and Z has a hard "zzz" sound. Practice making the "sss" and "zzz" sounds together.

4. ***Point*** at the word "roses" and say the word slowly. Ask, "Do you hear a soft S sound or a hard Z sound?" (Hard Z)

5. ***Point*** at the word "see," pronounce it slowly and ask, "Do you hear a soft S sound or a hard Z"? (Soft S)

Z z

bŭzz, bŭzz|ĕs

Writing Practice

weed　weed weed

rode　rode rode

pick　pick pick

rose　rose rose

roses　roses roses

buzz　buzz buzz

buzzes　buzzes buzzes

getting　getting getting

digging　digging digging

dropping　dropping dropping

The Red Rose

Bella picks a red rose.

She sticks the rose in Ann's hat.

The hat buzzes.

A small bee is in the rose.

New Words

1. Practice with your flash cards for the following letters. Show the letter side first, and ask for the letter sound. Do not show the picture side unless your student needs a hint.

Ă, Ĕ, Ĭ, Ŏ, Ŭ, Ô, Ē, Ō, Ī,
ST, W, P, SM, K, DR, CK,
SH, J, SW, ING, SL, OR, Z

stĭck
stĭcks
rĕd

Dandelion Fuzz

Ann and Bella go to see the roses.

They see a lot of dandelion weeds.

Ann picks a weed.

The dandelion has a ball of fuzz.

Four Syllables

1. _**Point**_ at the first new word and ask: "How many syllables does this word have?"

    (four)

2. Sound out the new words and read the story.

dăn|dē|lī|ŏn fŭzz

Fuzz Balls

Ann and Bella blow the fuzz off the dandelions.

The fuzz blows past the red roses.

Dan sees the fuzz.

They all blow the fuzz off the dandelions.

The BL Sound

1. ***Point*** at the block and explain that the letters B and L together sound like "bl" as in "block." Say the "bl" sound together.

2. ***Point*** at the new words and explain that they are sight words, but we can sound them out if we know that the O is long and the W is silent.

3. Sound out the new words and read the story.

4. ***Say*** the word "blows" slowly and ask "Do you hear a soft S sound or a hard Z sound?"

(Hard Z)

Bl, bl

blōw, blōws

Home With the Fuzz

An ant sees the fuzz.

He picks it all up.

He sticks it in his sack, so he can take it home.

He takes the fuzz home.

The Long A Sound

1. ***Point*** at the angel and say: "Long A sounds like 'ay' as in 'angel.'"

2. Return to page 8 and teach the long A section. Review the O, I and E sections.

3. ***Point*** at the new words and ask: "What vowels are in the new words?"

(Long A, Silent E, Long O)

4. Sound out the new words. Explain that the O in "so" is long because it's at the end of the word.

5. Read the story.

Ā
ā

tāke tākes, sō

The Ant Makes A Bed

The ant is going to make a bed so he can sleep.

He makes a bed of fuzz.

The ant is getting in his fuzz bed.

He is going to sleep.

Learning to Read - Long A

1. **_Ask:_** "What are the vowels in the new words?"

    (Long A and Silent E)

2. Sound out the new words.

3. **_Ask:_** "Where does a suffix go?"

    (On the end of a word)

4. **_Ask:_** "Which word has a suffix?"

    ("Makes" has the suffix "s")

5. Read the story.

6. **_Ask:_** "How do you spell 'on?'"

7. **_Ask:_** "How do you spell 'in?'"

8. **_Ask:_** "How do you spell 'to?'"

māke
mākes

Matt Jumped In

Matt went to the lake.

He ran to the end of the dock.

Then he jumped in the lake with his hat on.

Matt likes jumping off the dock.

New Words With Silent E

1. ***Point*** at the first new word and ask: "What does long A sound like?"

    (Like "ay" as in "angel")

2. Sound out the new words.

3. Read the story.

4. ***Ask:*** "How do you spell 'on?'"

5. ***Ask:*** "How do you spell 'in?'"

6. ***Ask:*** "How do you spell 'to?'"

7. ***Ask:*** "How many syllables are in 'jumped?'"

    (One)

Note: "Jumped" has one syllable because you can hear one vowel.

lāke
jŭmped

A Nap on the Dock

Matt's hat fell off in the lake.

His hat is all wet.

He gets up on the dock.

He takes a nap on the dock in the sun.

Review

1. Practice with your alphabet flash cards for the following letters. Show the letter side first, and ask for the letter sound. Do not show the picture side unless your student needs a hint.

Ă, Ĕ, Ĭ, Ŏ, Ŭ, Ô, Ē, Ō, Ī, Ā
ST, W, P, SM, K, DR, CK, J
SH, SW, ING, SL, OR, Z, BL

2. **_Ask:_** "How do you spell 'on?'"

3. **_Ask:_** "How do you spell 'in?'"

4. **_Ask:_** "How do you spell 'to?'"

Into the Lake

Dan rides his bike to the lake.

He sees Matt on the dock.

Dan ran onto the dock.

He jumped off the dock and into the lake.

More Compound Words

1. *Ask:* "How do you spell 'on?'"

2. *Ask:* "How do you spell 'in?'"

3. *Ask:* "How do you spell 'to?'"

4. *Point* at the new words say: "Both of these new words are compound words. That means they are really two smaller words put together."

5. Sound out the new words and read the story.

6. *Ask:* "How do you spell 'onto?'" "How to you spell 'into?'"

ŏn|to
ĭn|to

A Big Splash

Dan jumped in and made a big splash.

Matt woke up fast.

He got all wet.

He jumped into the lake to splash Dan back.

The SP Sound

1. ***Point*** at the spoon and explain that the consonants S and P together sound like "ssp" as in "spoon."

2. Sound out the new words.

3. Read the story.

splăsh
wōke
māde

Sp, sp

115

Writing Practice

fuzz fuzz fuzz

onto onto onto

splash splash splash

woke woke woke

make make make

take takes take takes

stick sticks stick sticks

blow blows blow blows

He jumped into the lake.
He jumped into the lake.

Kick and Splash

Dan uses his hands to splash Matt.

Matt uses his feet to splash Dan back.

They like to kick and splash a lot.

Swimming in the lake is so fun!

The Long U Sound

1. Return to page 8 and teach the U section. Review the A, E, I and O sections.

2. ***Point*** at the first new word and explain that the S has the hard Z sound, like "zzz" as in "zebra."

3. Sound out the first new word.

4. ***Point*** at the second new word and ask, "How many syllables does this word have?" (two)

5. Explain that the second new word has the hard Z sound for both S's.

6. Sound out the second new word and read the story.

Ū, ū

ūsȩ, ūs|ȇs

Ā, ā	take, takes, make, makes, lake wade, wades, sale, name, date, hate made, blade, shade, fade, trade same, blame, flame, ape, tape, late	
Ē, ē	he, she, see, sees, tree, be, we feet, bee, bees, feed, feeds, need sleep, seed, seeds, weed, weeds street, sweep, teen, seen, beep	
Ī, ī	tie, ties, hide, side, wide ride, rides, bike, like, likes, hike tire, fire, wire, shine, pine, fine, nine bite, kite, time, lime, dime, life, wife	
Ō, ō	hole, holes, hold, old, cold rose, roses, rode, rope woke, smoke, poke, joke home, bone, store, go, goes, pole	
Ū, ū	use, uses, cube, cute, mute, fuse tube, dude	
sl, bl	sleep, sled, slid, slip, slide black, blast, bless blow, blows, blame, bleed	

Long Vowels and Consonant Blends

1. The underlined words are for review.

2. Practice sounding out all the words on this page. If necessary, remind your student of the rules for two vowels together and Silent E.

3. Point out the hard and soft S's as you go.

4. Congratulations! You have finished Book 2! You may fill out the *Certificate of Achievement* on the next page, or go to BrodenBooks.com to download a free copy. Your student will be proud to show the certificate to friends and relatives.

156 New Words I Know

anthill, back, bad, bed, bee, bees, bike, bikes, bite, blow, blows, bone, bones, bus, buzz, buzzes, cannot, cold, dock, dandelion, digging, drop, drops, dropped, dropping, dump, eat, eats, end, fast, feed, feeds, feel, feels, feet, fell, fire, for, fuzz, getting, go, goes, going, had, he, her, him, hitting, hold, holds, hole, holes, home, hotdog, into, jump, jumped, jumping, jumps, junk, kick, kicked, kicks, kite, kites, lake, land, lands, lap, let, lets, like, likes, log, made, make, makes, nap, need, needed, needs, old, onto, past, pet, pick, picked, picks, picking, pothole, red, ride, rides, rock, rocks, rode, roll, rolled, rolling, rolls, rope, rose, roses, run, running, runs, sack, sad, see, seed, seeds, sees, she, shell, shells, shop, shopping, sleep, small, so, sold, splash, stick, sticks, stop, store, sun, sweep, sweeps, swim, swimming, swims, swing, swings, take, takes, then, they, tie, tied, ties, tire, tires, top, tosses, tree, up, use, uses, weed, weeds, went, wet, will, with, woke

Certificate of Achievement

I hereby certify that _____ has completed *REAL Phonics - Learn to Read, Book 2*, and is able to sound out all the words in the above list, except the four Sight Words (in red), which have been memorized.

_____

Signed by   Date

Alphabet Flash Cards

Color phonics flash cards are included at the back of each book in this reading program. Book 2 includes 52 flash cards for long and short vowels, consonants, consonant blends, diagraphs and sight words. There is no need for learning the letter sounds in advance, as the reading lesson plans will call for the flash cards as new letter sounds are introduced.

These flash cards will be your best tool for individualizing the study to suit the student. Some students will need extra time with all the flash cards, while others will need extra time with certain letters.

Important: Do not practice with the long vowel flash cards until the teacher's guide calls for it. Most children will confuse the long and short vowels if the long vowels are introduced too early, or before the child has had enough time to practice sounding out words with short vowels.

Long and Short Vowel Chart: As your student begins learning to sound out words with long vowels, he or she should review the appropriate section of the vowel chart on page 8. This will be much more useful than the flash cards for learning the silent E rule for long vowels.

Deluxe Flash Card Set for:
An Ant - Learn to Read, Book 1
Real Phonics - Learn to Read, Books 2-3

BrodenBooks.com is your source for the Deluxe Flash Card Set, which contains all of the flash cards for Books 1-3 in a single set. The Deluxe Set is printed on 4 x 6 inch durable coated card stock and is sturdy enough for classroom use. Here is a list of all the cards in the set:

Short Ă, Ĕ, Ĭ, Ŏ, Ŭ
Long Ā, Ē, Ī, Ō, Ū
Pointy Hat Ô

TH, ST, SM, DR, CK, SH, SW, ING
FL, SL, BL, SP, OR, TR, STR, BR
ÄR, OW, CL, GR, OU, GL, WH, SN
O̅O̅, CH, SK, ŎŎ

B, C, D, F, G, H, J, K, L, M, N, P, Q, R, S, T, V, W, X, Y, Z

Sight Word Flash Cards:
a, the, to, of, put, puts, blow, blows, laugh, laughs, want, wants, find, finds, what, where, do, you, give, gives, have, there, her, hers

Ă ă

B b

C c

D d

B b

A C

Q c

D d

C c

Ĕ ĕ

F f

G g

H h

F f

E e

H h

G g

Ĭ ĭ

J j

K k

L l

J

I

L

K

M m

N n

Ŏ ŏ

P p

N n

M m

P p

O o

Q q

R r

S s

T t

Qq

Ss

Rr

Tt

Ŭ ŭ

V v

Ww

Xx

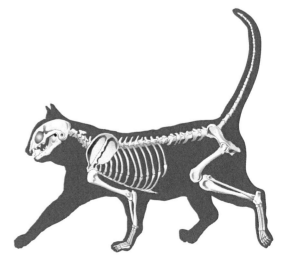

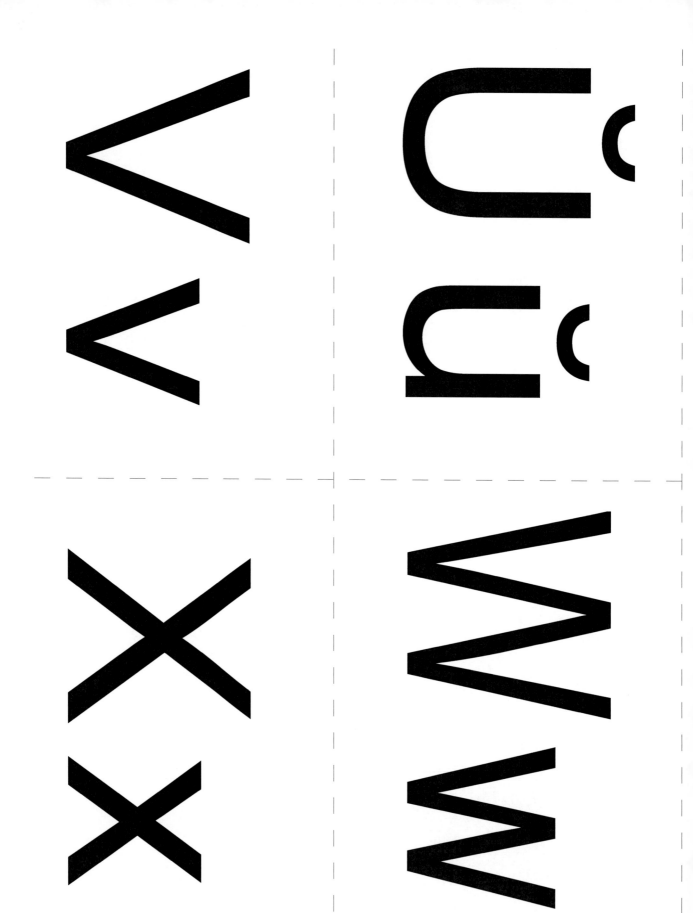

Y y

Z z

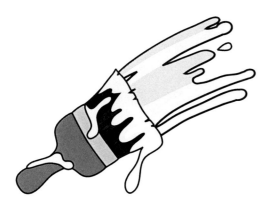

t h

Ô ô

Z z

Y y

O O

t h u

Ā ā

Ē ē

Ī ī

Ō ō

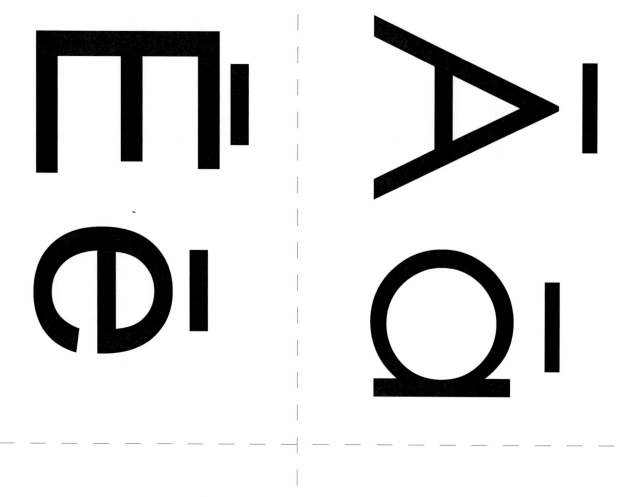
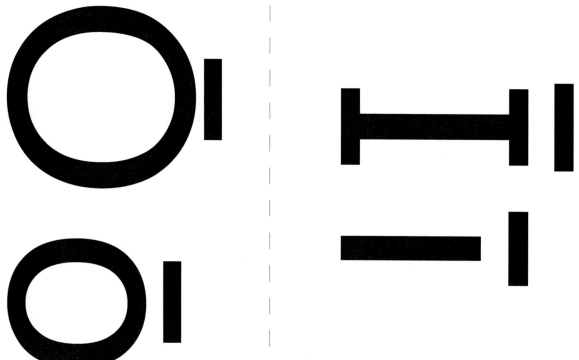

Ū ū

st

sm

dr

s t

ū n

u ū

d r

s m

n

ck

sh

sw

ing

s

h

c

k

i

ng

s

w

or

sl

bl

sp

s l

o r

s p

b l

blow

to

tr

of

they

the

tr

her

Made in the USA
San Bernardino, CA
01 November 2015